ULTIMATE DAD EXPERIENCE COUPONS

DAUGHTER EDITION

A Keepsake Journal of Father – Daughter Memories

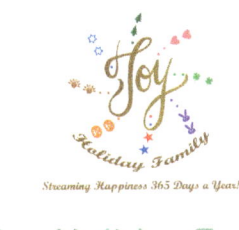

Joy Holiday Family

We do not remember days, we remember moments.

Cesare Pavese

Copyright © 2021 by Joy Holiday Family
All rights reserved. No part of this book may be reproduced or used in any manner without written permission of the copyright owner except for the use of quotations in a book review.

Book Design by Joy Holiday Publishing LLC

ISBN 978-1-7362873-6-1

Images used under license from Canva.com

Capture the MOMENTS
while you make the MEMORIES

You know your dad is special so get him the perfect gift! This book is the ultimate in father - daughter coupon gift-giving. Fifty-two thoughtful and entertaining coupons for daughters to give their dads. Enough coupons to have one for each week of the entire calendar year.

This keepsake journal is meant to chronicle not just the gift giving but the actual redemptions of the coupons. This gorgeous book takes the coupon idea to the next level. Each activity is designed as an elegant ticket. The large easy-to-read coupon tickets and redemption stubs are meant to stay in the book. Next to each coupon page is a space to place a photo and write what you did together.

There is also an additional page of smaller coupons replicating the larger tickets that may be cut out as part of the fun. This book is the solution to unused coupon books or gifts that are not part of a larger experience. Families can look back on all the special experiences they created together throughout the year.

With these coupon prompts dads get to spend quality time with their loved ones and time doing the things that they love on their own. This book includes activities for dads of all ages. We have even included some extra blank tickets since you know your father best. Is your dad a skydiving enthusiast, golfer, or gamer – you can fill in the blank!

We hope you'll use this book to create lots of beautiful moments together!

BEST DAD COUPON NO.01

BREAKFAST IN BED

007701

SIGN TO REDEEM

x _____ MONTH / DAY / YEAR

BEST DAD COUPON NO.02

NAP without interruption

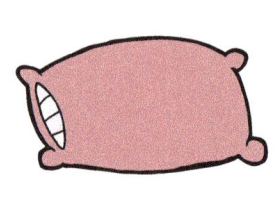

007702

SIGN TO REDEEM

x _____ MONTH / DAY / YEAR

BEST DAD COUPON NO.03

SLEEPING IN undisturbed

007703

SIGN TO REDEEM

x _____ MONTH / DAY / YEAR

HOW DID WE HAVE FUN?

Who

What

Where

BEST DAD COUPON NO.04

one day without **COMPLAINING**

007704
SIGN TO REDEEM
MONTH DAY YEAR

BEST DAD COUPON NO.05

one day filled with **COMPLIMENTS**

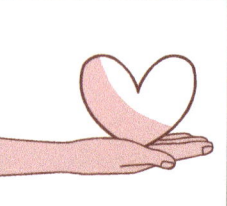

007705
SIGN TO REDEEM
MONTH DAY YEAR

BEST DAD COUPON NO.06

CALLING YOU "SIR"
all day long,
or the title of your choice

HOW DID WE HAVE FUN?

Who

What

Where

BEST DAD COUPON NO.07

PERSONAL ASSISTANT
for the day

007707

SIGN TO REDEEM

x _____

MONTH | DAY | YEAR

BEST DAD COUPON NO.08

listen to & laugh at
1 DAD JOKE

007708

SIGN TO REDEEM

x _____

MONTH | DAY | YEAR

BEST DAD COUPON NO.09

attentively listen to 1 session of
DAD ADVICE

007709

SIGN TO REDEEM

x _____

MONTH | DAY | YEAR

HOW DID WE HAVE FUN?

Who

What

Where

BEST DAD COUPON NO.10

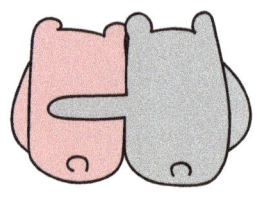
give you one gigantic **BEAR HUG**

007710
SIGN TO REDEEM

BEST DAD COUPON NO.11

DANCE PARTY

007711
SIGN TO REDEEM

BEST DAD COUPON NO.12

house & car **DJ FOR THE DAY**

007712
SIGN TO REDEEM

HOW DID WE HAVE FUN?

Who

What

Where

BEST DAD COUPON NO.13

CAR DETAIL
clean the inside of your ride

007713
SIGN TO REDEEM
x _____
MONTH DAY YEAR

BEST DAD COUPON NO.14

CAR WASH
by hand

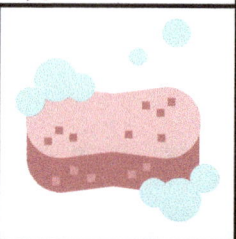

007714
SIGN TO REDEEM
x _____
MONTH DAY YEAR

BEST DAD COUPON NO.15

assist you with
YARD WORK

007715
SIGN TO REDEEM
x _____
MONTH DAY YEAR

HOW DID WE HAVE FUN?

Who

What

Where

BEST DAD COUPON NO.16

TAKE OUT THE TRASH

007716
SIGN TO REDEEM
MONTH DAY YEAR

BEST DAD COUPON NO.17

GO FOR A WALK
together

007717
SIGN TO REDEEM
MONTH DAY YEAR

BEST DAD COUPON NO.18

OUTDOOR CHORE
of your choice

007718
SIGN TO REDEEM
MONTH DAY YEAR

HOW DID WE HAVE FUN?

Who

What

Where

BEST DAD COUPON NO.19

★ ★ ★ ★ ★ ★ ★ ★ ★ ★ ★ ★ ★

 wash, dry, & fold
YOUR LAUNDRY

007719
SIGN TO REDEEM
x _____
MONTH DAY YEAR

BEST DAD COUPON NO.20

★ ★ ★ ★ ★ ★ ★ ★ ★ ★ ★ ★ ★

CHORE
of your choice

007720
SIGN TO REDEEM
x _____
MONTH DAY YEAR

BEST DAD COUPON NO.21

★ ★ ★ ★ ★ ★ ★ ★ ★ ★ ★ ★ ★

 **ORGANIZE**
your _____

007721
SIGN TO REDEEM
x _____
MONTH DAY YEAR

HOW DID WE HAVE FUN?

Who

What

Where

BEST DAD COUPON NO.22

MASTER OF THE REMOTE CONTROL
for 1 day

007722
SIGN TO REDEEM
MONTH DAY YEAR

BEST DAD COUPON NO.23

MOVIE NIGHT
movie of your choice

007723
SIGN TO REDEEM
MONTH DAY YEAR

BEST DAD COUPON NO.24

uninterrupted
GAMING

007724
SIGN TO REDEEM
MONTH DAY YEAR

HOW DID WE HAVE FUN?

Who

What

Where

BEST DAD COUPON NO.25

BOARD GAME
of your choice

007725

SIGN TO REDEEM

MONTH DAY YEAR

x

BEST DAD COUPON NO.26

OUTDOOR GAME
of your choice

007726

SIGN TO REDEEM

MONTH DAY YEAR

x

BEST DAD COUPON NO.27

VIDEO GAME
of your choice

007727

SIGN TO REDEEM

MONTH DAY YEAR

x

HOW DID WE HAVE FUN?

Who

What

Where

BEST DAD COUPON NO. 28

OUTDOOR ADVENTURE

007728

SIGN TO REDEEM

BEST DAD COUPON NO. 29

BUILD 1 THING TOGETHER

007729

SIGN TO REDEEM

BEST DAD COUPON NO. 30

FIX 1 THING TOGETHER

007730

SIGN TO REDEEM

HOW DID WE HAVE FUN?

Who

What

Where

BEST DAD COUPON NO.31

★ ★ ★ ★ ★ ★ ★ ★ ★ ★ ★ ★ ★

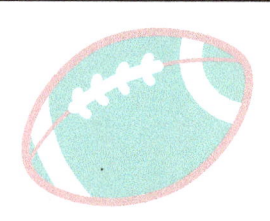

WATCH YOUR
FAVE SPORT
at home

007731

SIGN TO REDEEM

x _____

MONTH | DAY | YEAR

BEST DAD COUPON NO.32

★ ★ ★ ★ ★ ★ ★ ★ ★ ★ ★ ★ ★

WATCH YOUR
FAVE SPORT
in person

007732

SIGN TO REDEEM

x _____

MONTH | DAY | YEAR

BEST DAD COUPON NO.33

★ ★ ★ ★ ★ ★ ★ ★ ★ ★ ★ ★ ★

PLAY CATCH

007733

SIGN TO REDEEM

x _____

MONTH | DAY | YEAR

HOW DID WE HAVE FUN?

Who

What

Where

BEST DAD COUPON NO.34

TAKEOUT DINNER
of your choice

007734

SIGN TO REDEEM

x _____

MONTH DAY YEAR

BEST DAD COUPON NO.35

HOMEMADE MEAL
of your choice

007735

SIGN TO REDEEM

x _____

MONTH DAY YEAR

BEST DAD COUPON NO.36

MAKE HOMEMADE PIZZA
together

007736

HOW DID WE HAVE FUN?

Who

What

Where

BEST DAD COUPON NO. 37

BAKE
FAVORITE COOKIES
together

007737
SIGN TO REDEEM
x _____
MONTH | DAY | YEAR

BEST DAD COUPON NO. 38

BAKE
FAVORITE CAKE
for you

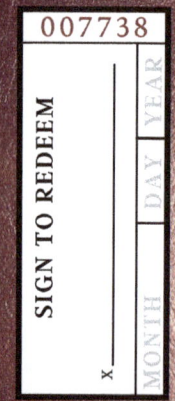

007738
SIGN TO REDEEM
x _____
MONTH | DAY | YEAR

BEST DAD COUPON NO. 39

COFFEE OF
YOUR CHOICE

007739
SIGN TO REDEEM
x _____
MONTH | DAY | YEAR

HOW DID WE HAVE FUN?

Who
What
Where

BEST DAD COUPON NO.40

RESTAURANT
of your choice

007740
SIGN TO REDEEM
x _____
MONTH DAY YEAR

BEST DAD COUPON NO.41

take you out to
ICE CREAM

007741
SIGN TO REDEEM
x _____
MONTH DAY YEAR

BEST DAD COUPON NO.42

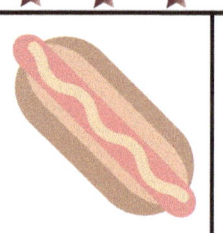

FOOD TRUCK
of your choice

007742
SIGN TO REDEEM
x _____
MONTH DAY YEAR

HOW DID WE HAVE FUN?

Who

What

Where

BEST DAD COUPON NO. 43

BRING IN THE MAIL

007743
SIGN TO REDEEM
x _____
MONTH DAY YEAR

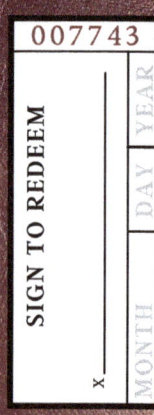

BEST DAD COUPON NO. 44

DO HOMEWORK
without complaining

007744
SIGN TO REDEEM
x _____
MONTH DAY YEAR

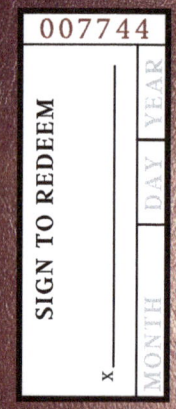

BEST DAD COUPON NO. 45

sort your
SOCK DRAWER

007745
SIGN TO REDEEM
x _____
MONTH DAY YEAR

HOW DID WE HAVE FUN?

Who

What

Where

BEST DAD COUPON NO. 46

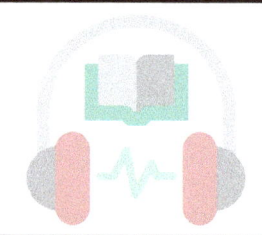

LISTEN TO AN AUDIOBOOK
together

007746
SIGN TO REDEEM
MONTH DAY YEAR

BEST DAD COUPON NO. 47

EXERCISE OF YOUR CHOICE
together

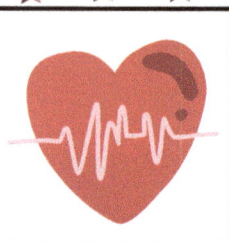

007747
SIGN TO REDEEM
MONTH DAY YEAR

BEST DAD COUPON NO. 48

go to a CAR SHOW

007748
SIGN TO REDEEM
MONTH DAY YEAR

HOW DID WE HAVE FUN?

Who

What

Where

BEST DAD COUPON NO.49

first pick of the
HALLOWEEN CANDY HAUL

007749
SIGN TO REDEEM
x _____
MONTH DAY YEAR

BEST DAD COUPON NO.50

BUILD A SNOWMAN together

007750
SIGN TO REDEEM
x _____
MONTH DAY YEAR

BEST DAD COUPON NO.51

MAKE POPSICLES together

007751
SIGN TO REDEEM
x _____
MONTH DAY YEAR

HOW DID WE HAVE FUN?

Who

What

Where

BEST DAD COUPON NO.52

★ ★ ★ ★ ★ ★ ★ ★ ★ ★ ★ ★ ★ ★ ★

I will be happy to:
_____
_____

007752
SIGN TO REDEEM
x _____
MONTH DAY YEAR

BEST DAD COUPON NO.53

★ ★ ★ ★ ★ ★ ★ ★ ★ ★ ★ ★ ★ ★ ★

I will be happy to:
_____
_____

007753
SIGN TO REDEEM
x _____
MONTH DAY YEAR

BEST DAD COUPON NO.54

★ ★ ★ ★ ★ ★ ★ ★ ★ ★ ★ ★ ★ ★ ★

I will be happy to:
_____
_____

007754
SIGN TO REDEEM
x _____
MONTH DAY YEAR

HOW DID WE HAVE FUN?

Who

What

Where